DO YOU KNOW?

Level 2

AT SEA

Written by Hannah Fish
Series Editor: Nick Coates

LADYBIRD BOOKS

UK | USA | Canada | Ireland | Australia
India | New Zealand | South Africa

Ladybird Books is part of the Penguin Random House group of companies
whose addresses can be found at global.penguinrandomhouse.com.
www.penguin.co.uk   www.puffin.co.uk   www.ladybird.co.uk

Penguin
Random House
UK

First published 2021
001

Text copyright © Ladybird Books Ltd, 2021
Illustrations by Dynamo Limited
Illustrations copyright © Ladybird Books Ltd, 2021

Printed in China

The authorized representative in the EEA is Penguin Random House Ireland, Morrison Chambers, 32 Nassau Street, Dublin D02 YH68
A CIP catalogue record for this book is available from the British Library

ISBN: 978–0–241–50339–3

All correspondence to:
Ladybird Books
Penguin Random House Children's
One Embassy Gardens, 8 Viaduct Gardens, London SW11 7BW

Contents

New words

air

engine

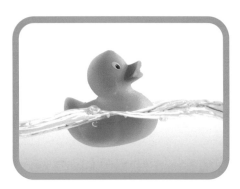

float
(verb)

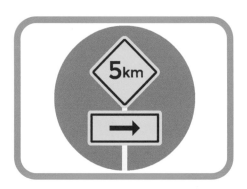

kilometre

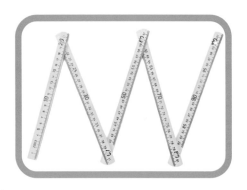

metre

move
(verb)

oil

propeller

shape
(noun)

ship

steer

wave
(noun)

What makes waves?

The water in the sea is always **moving**. Wind moves across the sea and makes **waves**. Some waves are very big. People can ride these waves on a surfboard.

fin

The surfboard moves with the wave. It has a fin. The fin helps the person **steer**, and stay on the wave.

The sun and the moon can move the sea. They make waves, too.

moon

sun

surfboard

PROJECT

Work with a friend.
1 Find a plastic bottle. **2** Fill ½ of your bottle with water and blue food colouring. **3** Fill the rest of the container up with vegetable oil. **4** Close your bottle, and roll it on a table! Watch the waves move in your sea.

How do boats move?

Boats **float** on water. Oars can make a boat travel quickly. Some boats have lots of oars!

rowing boat

Oars can steer a boat, too. Move the right oar, and the boat goes left.

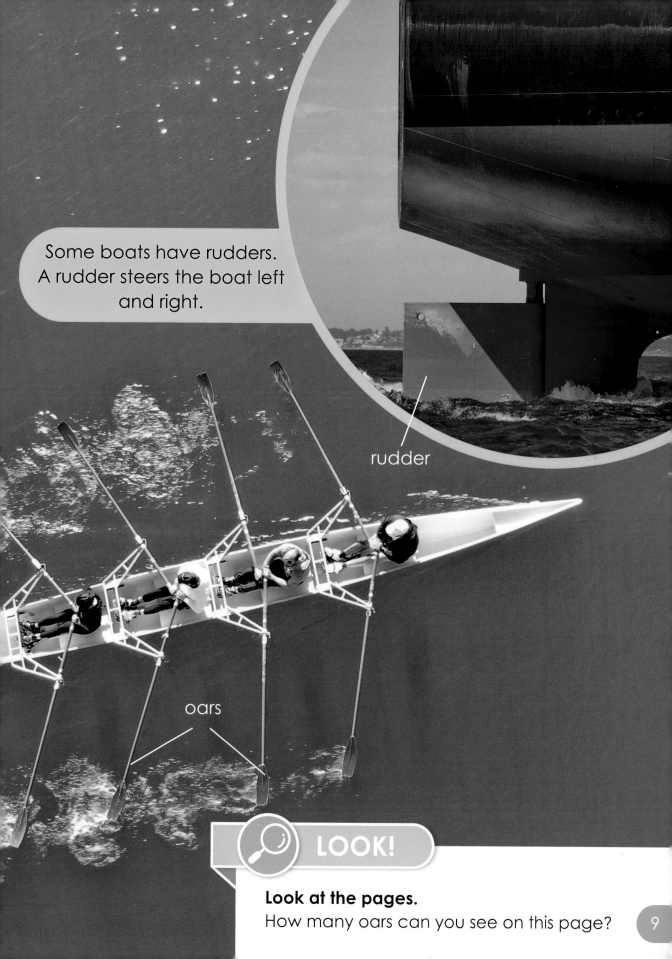

Some boats have rudders. A rudder steers the boat left and right.

rudder

oars

LOOK!

Look at the pages.
How many oars can you see on this page?

9

What does a sail do?

Many boats have sails. Wind hits the sails and moves the boat. Some boats have lots of sails.

sail

In strong winds, sailboats can travel fast.

This windsurfer has a sail. The wind makes it travel fast. Moving the sail steers the windsurfer!

FIND OUT!

Use books or the internet to find out how a sailboat can move into the wind.

How do engines move a boat?

A boat's **engine** moves a **propeller** under the water.

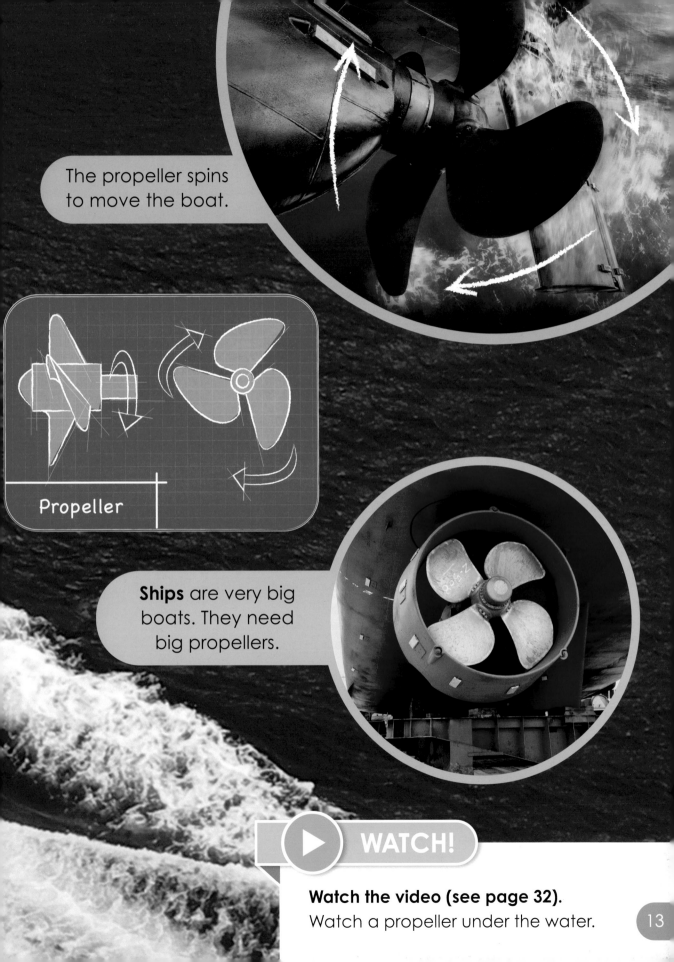

The propeller spins to move the boat.

Propeller

Ships are very big boats. They need big propellers.

▶ **WATCH!**

Watch the video (see page 32).
Watch a propeller under the water.

How fast are boats?

Speedboats move very fast. They have engines and propellers. The **shape** of this speedboat helps it move fast.

The Spirit of Australia is a very fast speedboat. It can travel at 510 **kilometres** an hour.

We can use fast boats for sports. This woman is water-skiing.

water-skiing

FIND OUT!

Use books or the internet to find out about the Spirit of Australia. Who made it? When did they use it?

How big are ships?

Some ships are very big. They can carry heavy things across the sea. Look at this big ship. It is carrying lots of boxes.

The Seawise Giant was a very big ship. It was 458 **metres** long!

You can have a holiday on a ship. This is a cruise ship, it can carry 8,000 people. It has 23 restaurants, too!

THINK!

Do you want to travel on a cruise ship? Why? Why not?

What is a catamaran?

Catamarans are a different shape to other boats. They have two hulls. This means they float very well.

hull

rudders

Catamarans need two rudders for steering. There is one on each hull.

Catamarans are not heavy, and they can move fast. They are good boats for sport.

ENERGY OBSERVER

PROJECT

Work with a friend.
Make a catamaran with two plastic bottles.
Put it in the sink. Does it float?

Can we drive on the sea?

Boats float on the sea, but hovercrafts float in the **air** above the sea. Some hovercrafts are small and carry one person. But some hovercrafts are big and carry lots of people.

Under the hovercraft there is air. The hovercraft moves on the air above the sea.

Hovercrafts can drive on water and on land.

land

This car can drive on the road and in the sea.

www.jokulsarlon.is

KLAKI

▶ WATCH!

Watch the video (see page 32).
How does a car drive from the land into water?

Do people live at sea?

Look at this platform out at sea. People live and work on sea platforms. Their job is to get **oil** from under the sea floor. There is a lot of oil under the sea.

platform

There are pipes in the sea under the platform. The pipes go into the sea floor.

cabin

pipes

Bedrooms at sea are called cabins.

FIND OUT!

Use books or the internet to find out about life on a sea platform. How long do people live and work on the platform for?

How do we travel under the sea?

A submarine is a boat but it travels under the sea! Submarines have air tanks. They go down and up using air and water.

submarine

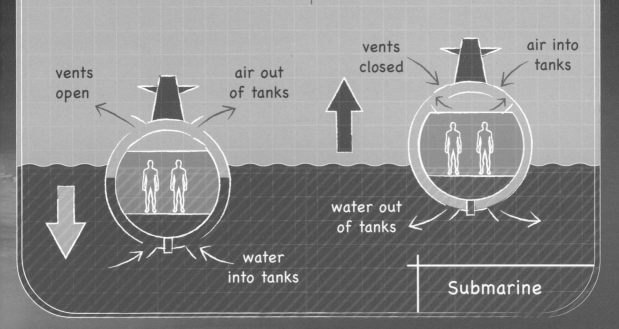

1. Air goes out of the air tanks and water comes in. The submarine goes DOWN.

2. Air goes into the air tanks and water comes out. The submarine goes UP.

vents open

air out of tanks

vents closed

air into tanks

water into tanks

water out of tanks

Submarine

Look inside a submarine!

PROJECT

Cornelis Drebbel made the first submarine in 1620. Find out about this submarine and make a poster about it.

What lives under the sea?

Many plants and animals live under the sea. We can learn about sea plants and animals using a submersible.

submersible

This is a diver. They can swim under the sea in a diving suit. The diving suit gives the diver air.

diver

diving suit

Divers take photos of sea plants and animals.

We can watch sea animals in a submersible.

THINK!

Which animals live under the sea? What is your favourite sea animal?

Can people live under the sea?

Aquarius is 9 kilometres under the sea. Six people can live and work in Aquarius. They live there for two weeks, and they study sea plants and animals.

Aquarius

This person is living and working on Aquarius.

We do not have cities under the sea yet, but people are thinking about them.

PROJECT

Work with a friend.
Think about a city under the sea. What things would you like in your city? Draw a picture of your underwater city.

Quiz

Choose the correct answers.

1 Rudders . . . in water
to steer a boat.
a catch
b swim
c move

2 Sails use . . . to move a boat.
a the wind
b the sea
c the sun

3 . . . can move very fast.
a Kayaks
b Surfboards
c Speedboats

4 Catamarans are . . . because
they float really well.
a heavy
b safe
c fast

5 Hovercrafts travel . . . the sea.
   a under
   b above
   c on

6 People . . . on sea platforms.
   a live and work
   b float and drive
   c swim and windsurf

7 We can watch . . . in a submersible.
   a people
   b sea animals
   c ships

8 People live in Aquarius
for about . . .
   a two weeks.
   b twenty days.
   c thirty days.

DO YOU KNOW?

Visit www.ladybirdeducation.co.uk for
FREE **DO YOU KNOW?** teaching resources.

- video clips with simplified voiceover and subtitles
- video and comprehension activities
- class projects and lesson plans
- audio recording of every book
- digital version of every book
- full answer keys

To access video clips, audio tracks and digital books:

1 Go to **www.ladybirdeducation.co.uk**
2 Click "Unlock book"
3 Enter the code below

kP3WMxWTtD

Stay safe online! Some of the DO YOU KNOW? activities ask children to do extra research online. Remember:

- ensure an adult is supervising;
- use established search engines such as Google or Kiddle;
- children should never share personal details, such as name, home or school address, telephone number or photos.